THE AMERICAN PRESIDENTS

A FOLD—OUT VINYL STICKER BOOK

Reader's Digest
Children's Books®

New York, New York • Montréal, Québec • Bath, United Kingdom

★ CONTENTS ★

★ INTRODUCTION ★

*"I do solemnly swear that I will faithfully execute
the Office of the President of the United States,
and will to the best of my Ability,
preserve, protect and defend
the Constitution of the United States."*

With these simple words, every four years, one person takes on the hardest job in the world—President of the United States of America.

What are the duties? Enforce every federal law of the land. Approve or disapprove every new law the Congress makes. Meet with the leaders of other nations and find ways to get along. Run the largest and most powerful military in history and, if necessary, lead it to war.

To do the job right, you need extraordinary skill at striking deals and making agreements between people who rarely agree on anything. It also helps to be an excellent speech maker, not only to inspire the nation and show it the way, but to get it to follow. One other part of the job: When anything goes wrong, you usually get the blame.

What are the qualifications? On paper, not much. You must be a natural-born U.S. citizen, at least 35 years old, and you must have lived in the United States for at least fourteen years. Other than that, anyone is eligible.

The President of the United States has tremendous power, but that power is not unlimited. The last thing our Founding Fathers wanted was another king. The President, for instance, can only serve two terms and cannot make new laws. Making new laws is Congress's job. And the President cannot decide what a particular law is trying to say—that is the job of the courts.

So, picture a triangle. In the three corners you have President, Congress, and the Courts keeping an eye on each other, neither one letting another get too powerful. This is called a system of checks and balances, and it is tug-of-war, arm wrestling, chess, poker, and staring contest all rolled into one.

No one said being CEO of the USA was easy. As President Eisenhower put it: "No easy problems ever come to the President of the United States. If they are easy to solve, somebody else has solved them."

Over the past 223 years, forty-four men have taken on the challenge. Of those forty-four, nine (including some of the greatest) never went to college; nearly half had never worked in Washington before; nine were born poor in log cabins; others were from very rich families; eight were born subjects of the English king; four were murdered in office; six were attacked and almost killed; and four died on the job of natural causes.

One was never married; one was married in the White House; one had fifteen children and one had only an adopted son. The tallest was six-foot-four, the shortest was five-foot-four. The oldest was 69, the youngest was 42.

All had great hopes. Some did brilliant jobs, some were just so-so. Several were good, and a few—through bumbling, cheating, or overstepping their authority—were downright bad. Two—almost three—were put on trial by the Senate. But a few have been truly great leaders, making our nation bigger, stronger, saving not only the United States, but the world.

"The presidency has made every man who occupied it, no matter how small, bigger than he was," said President Lyndon Johnson, "and no matter how big, not big enough for its demands."

Each of the American presidents was a bigger-than-life celebrity in his time. The whole world was watching. Not because of their glamour or power, but because they had been put at the controls of one of the greatest experiments in history—the experiment to see if people really can get along without kings and emperors and dictators telling them what to do, if people really can rule themselves with freedom and justice for everyone—the experiment called the United States.

These are the forty-four men who have passed that unfolding experiment on to us.

Let's meet them.

GEORGE WASHINGTON
1st PRESIDENT ★ 1789 – 1797
Father of His Country

"I can foresee that nothing but the rooting out of slavery can perpetuate the existence of our union."

★ AT A GLANCE ★

BORN
February 22, 1732
Pope's Creek, Virginia

POLITICAL PARTY
Federalist

VICE PRESIDENT
John Adams

FIRST LADY
Martha

CHILDREN
John "Jacky"
and Martha "Patsy"

PETS
Vulcan, Madame Moose,
Sweet Lips, and Searcher,
all hounds

When General George Washington's army defeated the British in the Revolutionary War, some of the officers began talking about the possibility of making Washington king of America. Washington hated the idea.

At six-foot-two, 200 pounds, Washington was a big man. He wore size 13 boots. He had reddish-blond hair, and terrible problems with his teeth. He continually experimented with different kinds of false teeth made from ivory, hippo teeth, lead and even recycled his own teeth.

Washington loved the outdoors, fishing and foxhunting especially. As a young man, he worked as a surveyor, hiking across all kinds of rugged colonial American landscapes.

He never had any children of his own, but his wife, Martha, had two young children—"Jacky" and "Patsy"—from her first marriage and he raised them as his own. As far as formal schooling went, he never went beyond grammar school and always had trouble spelling. But he did have an IQ of 125.

Seventeen cities, thirty-one counties, one state, and our nation's capital are named after Washington. He is considered one of our greatest presidents because he saw our nation through one of its most difficult times—its birth.

JOHN ADAMS
2nd PRESIDENT ★ 1797 – 1801
Atlas of Independence

Born and raised outside of Boston, John Adams graduated from Harvard College in 1755. His great-great-grandparents were among the Pilgrims who landed on Plymouth Rock in 1620. When he was elected president, the nation's capital was still in Philadelphia. When the new capital, including the White House, was ready in Washington, D.C., in 1800, President Adams became the first president to live there. He wrote: "May none but honest and wise men ever rule under this roof."

In those days, the candidate getting the second most votes became vice president. That's how Thomas Jefferson became Adams's vice president. The two men frequently argued about what the brand-new government should be. Adams wanted the government to grow bigger and have a big army, and to raise taxes to pay for it all. Jefferson wanted government to stay small. Adams and Jefferson were so angry at each other that when Jefferson beat Adams in the next election, Adams did not go to his swearing-in ceremony. Years later, the two Founding Fathers became friends again.

Adams and Jefferson were the only two presidents who signed the Declaration of Independence, which Jefferson wrote. Strangely enough, Adams and Jefferson died within hours of each other on the same day, July 4, 1826, the Declaration's 50th anniversary.

"I must study politics and war that my sons may have liberty to study mathematics and philosophy."

★ AT A GLANCE ★

BORN
October 30, 1735
Quincy, Massachusetts

POLITICAL PARTY
Federalist

VICE PRESIDENT
Thomas Jefferson

FIRST LADY
Abigail

CHILDREN
Abigail, John Quincy, Susanna, Charles, and Thomas

PETS
Cleopatra, a horse; Juno and Satan, dogs

THOMAS JEFFERSON
3rd PRESIDENT ★ 1801 – 1809
The Sage of Monticello

"Every generation needs a new revolution."

★ AT A GLANCE ★

BORN
April 13, 1743
Shadwell, Virginia

POLITICAL PARTY
Democratic-Republican

VICE PRESIDENTS
Aaron Burr;
George Clinton

FIRST LADY
Martha

CHILDREN
Martha, Mary,
and four children who
died in infancy

PETS
Mockingbird, dogs,
horses, and bears

After he was sworn in as president in 1801, Thomas Jefferson walked across the street to a boardinghouse to get some dinner. There were no empty seats, so he waited. When he moved into the White House, he stopped one custom that General Washington had started—the president bowing to visitors. Jefferson began shaking hands instead.

Jefferson did not like stuffiness or fancy clothes. His idea of an enjoyable evening was to have people over to talk about books and ideas. His collection of 6,000 volumes became the first Library of Congress.

In 1803, he bought the vast territory of Louisiana from France, doubling the size of our country, for a mere $15 million. Then he sent his Virginia neighbor's son, Meriwether Lewis, and Captain William Clark to explore the area and try to find a boat route to the Pacific Ocean.

Jefferson liked to invent things. The swivel chair, a letter-copying machine, and the dumbwaiter were just some of his ideas. He played the violin, spoke six languages, and taught himself architecture. You can still visit his home, Monticello, and the nearby University of Virginia, both of which he designed and built.

Although he owned slaves, Jefferson realized that the evil of slavery would be one of the biggest problems our nation would have to solve. In 1808, he banned the importation of slaves from Africa.

JAMES MADISON
4th PRESIDENT ★ 1809 – 1817
Father of the Constitution

One of only two presidents (along with Washington) who signed the U.S. Constitution—the set of rules and laws for governing our country—James Madison never thought the Constitution went far enough to protect individual rights. So, when he became president, he pushed Congress to pass the Bill of Rights (the first ten amendments), which spells out and guarantees things like freedom of speech, freedom of religion, and the right to a trial by jury if someone's accused of a crime.

And even though the British had surrendered in the Revolution, they hadn't really given up. On the high seas, they kept stealing U.S. ships and cargo, and even kidnapped our sailors and forced them to serve in the British navy. By 1812, the United States had had enough and President Madison declared war on England.

At first, the War of 1812 didn't go too well. The British invaded Washington and even burned the White House. America eventually won the war.

At five-foot-four and 100 pounds, Madison was the smallest of all the presidents, but he was the first to stop wearing knickers and start wearing long pants. After two terms, he retired to his home in Virginia and helped Thomas Jefferson build the University of Virginia and work to end slavery.

"If men were angels, no government would be necessary."

★ AT A GLANCE ★

BORN
March 16, 1751
Port Conway, Virginia

POLITICAL PARTY
Democratic-Republican

VICE PRESIDENTS
George Clinton;
Elbridge Gerry

FIRST LADY
Dolley

PET
A green parrot
belonging to
Mrs. Madison

JAMES MONROE
5th PRESIDENT ★ 1817 – 1825
Era of Good Feelings

"Our country may be likened to a new house. We lack many things, but we possess the most precious of all—liberty!"

★ AT A GLANCE ★

BORN
April 28, 1758
Westmoreland County,
Virginia

POLITICAL PARTY
Democratic-Republican

VICE PRESIDENT
Daniel D. Tompkins

FIRST LADY
Elizabeth

CHILDREN
Eliza, James, and Maria

PET
A spaniel belonging
to Maria

James Monroe's parents died when he was a teenager, and he was in college at William and Mary in Williamsburg, Virginia, when the Revolutionary War started. He was just 17 when he and some classmates raided the British armory at the Governor's Mansion and got away with 200 muskets and 300 swords, which they sneaked to the Virginia militia.

Monroe became an officer in Washington's army when he was 18. He was with General Washington when he crossed the Delaware and during that dreadful winter at Valley Forge. He was nearly killed capturing British cannons at Trenton, New Jersey.

After the war, Monroe joined Thomas Jefferson's law practice. By the time Monroe ran for president, our young country was enjoying an economic boom. The good times did not last, however. In 1819, we had an economic depression. Monroe's administration was also marked by a debate whether or not to let Missouri join the United States as a slave state or as a non-slave state, and the purchase of Florida from Spain. During his two terms, the number of states in the United States increased from fifteen to twenty-four.

He was also known for the Monroe Doctrine, which basically warned European kings and queens to not even think about starting new colonies in either North—or South—America!

JOHN QUINCY ADAMS
6th PRESIDENT ★ 1825 – 1829
Old Man Elephant

When he was 8 years old, John Quincy Adams watched the Battle of Bunker Hill from his farm near Boston. At 10 he traveled with his father, John Adams, to Europe and learned to speak French and Dutch. While he was still a teenager, he got a job with the U.S. embassy in Russia. When he came home and graduated from Harvard, he figured his career would be in international diplomacy.

He was an ambassador under President Washington and under his father, the second president; a U.S. senator under President Jefferson; an ambassador for President Madison; and secretary of state under President Monroe.

Being president of the United States was his least favorite job. He wanted the government to start building lots of bridges and roads so our country could grow and prosper, but he couldn't convince Congress to spend the money. Why? He refused to play party politics, making deals and promises and trades for this and that. He stuck instead to his principles and ended up making lots of enemies.

Since he did not campaign for a second term, he lost re-election. But then he ran for Congress, and that job he loved. He fought hard to force Congress to find a way to solve the problem of slavery. He collapsed and eventually died in his beloved Capitol building.

"If your actions inspire others to dream more, learn more, do more, and become more, you are a leader."

★ AT A GLANCE ★

BORN
July 11, 1767
Braintree (now Quincy),
Massachusetts

POLITICAL PARTY
Federalist, Democratic-Republican, and Whig

VICE PRESIDENT
John C. Calhoun

FIRST LADY
Louisa

CHILDREN
George Washington, John, Charles, and Louisa

PET
An alligator

ANDREW JACKSON
7th PRESIDENT ★ 1829 – 1837
Old Hickory

"Americans are not a perfect people, but we are called to a perfect mission."

★ **AT A GLANCE** ★

BORN
March 15, 1767
Waxhaw,
North-South Carolina
border

POLITICAL PARTY
Democrat

VICE PRESIDENTS
John C. Calhoun;
Martin Van Buren

FIRST LADY
Rachel

CHILDREN
Andrew Jackson, Jr.
(adopted)

PETS
Several horses, including
Sam Patches, his war horse

Andrew Jackson was the first U.S. president who was born in a log cabin. His parents were poor immigrants from Northern Ireland. Very few of their neighbors in South Carolina could read, so in 1776, when he was just 9 years old, Andrew read the Declaration of Independence out loud for everyone to hear.

When the Revolutionary War broke out, Andrew and his brother joined the militia cavalry in North Carolina. He was only 13, so they made him a messenger. Unfortunately, he was captured and when a mean British officer ordered him to polish his boots, Andrew refused. The officer pulled out his sword and slashed Andrew across the face. He wore the scar proudly for the rest of his life.

In 1806, a man named Charles Dickinson insulted Jackson's wife, so Jackson challenged him to a duel. Dickinson fired and his bullet lodged near Jackson's heart without killing him. When Jackson fired, Dickinson did not survive.

Jackson rejoined the military for the War of 1812 and clobbered the British in the Battle of New Orleans, becoming  a two-star general and war hero. As president, Jackson was criticized for firing his enemies from government jobs and for not doing what Congress wanted him to do. Critics called him "King Andrew," but he did make the office of president stronger than it had ever been before.

MARTIN VAN BUREN
8th PRESIDENT ★ 1837 – 1841
The Little Magician

Even though he was the first president born in the United States (all the ones before him were born when America was still a British colony), Martin Van Buren spoke Dutch at home. His father ran a tavern in Kinderhook, New York, in between New York City and the state capital, Albany. People stopping for the night were

always talking politics and young Martin got interested. His father couldn't afford to send him to law school, but did get him a job as a clerk in a law office. He taught himself the law and became a lawyer.

Van Buren liked the idea of keeping the government small. For that reason, and because he was famous for being good at settling arguments and getting people to agree (why he got the nickname "Little Magician"), he was asked by Andrew Jackson to be vice president.

Jackson was very popular when he left office and only had to endorse Van Buren to get him elected. But soon the country's economy took a nosedive and his new nickname became "Martin Van Ruin."

The two happiest days of his life, he once said, were the day he became president and the day he left the presidency. He spent the rest of his days fighting against slavery.

"It is easier to do a job right than to explain why you didn't."

★ AT A GLANCE ★

BORN
December 5, 1782
Kinderhook, New York

POLITICAL PARTY
Democrat

VICE PRESIDENT
Richard M. Johnson

FIRST LADY
Hannah

CHILDREN
Abraham, John, Martin, Winfield (died in first year), and Smith

PETS
A pair of tiger cubs

WILLIAM HENRY HARRISON
9th PRESIDENT ★ 1841
Old Tippecanoe

"The people are the best guardians of their own rights."

Often called a tragic figure, William Henry Harrison studied medicine, but became a soldier. His most famous battle was in 1811 against warriors of the Shawnee nation on the banks of the Tippecanoe River. Neither side really won the battle, but the Shawnee chief, Tecumseh, got so angry at the U.S. soldiers for giving whiskey to his people that—as the legend supposedly goes—he put a curse on our government: Every president elected in a year ending in a zero would die in office.

Harrison was nicknamed for that battle, so when he ran for president and picked John Tyler as his running mate, their slogan became "Tippecanoe and Tyler Too!" Although he was from a wealthy Virginia background, his campaign managers put the word out that just like Andrew Jackson, Harrison had also been born poor in a log cabin. Guided by his strategists, Harrison avoided talking about any important issues, a campaign tactic that worked and sadly has been imitated too much ever since.

At 67, Harrison was the oldest man yet to be elected president, but, tragically, only four of his ten children lived long enough to see him win the presidency. He was inaugurated outside on a bitterly cold day, gave a speech that dragged on for an hour and forty minutes (the longest ever), caught pneumonia, and died a month later—the first president to die in office.

JOHN TYLER
10th PRESIDENT ★ 1841 – 1845
His Accidency

When President Harrison died thirty-one days after being sworn into office, his vice president, John Tyler, became the first man to step into the office of president without being elected. Many people argued that he should not have all the powers of an elected president. They called him "His Accidency." Harrison's cabinet thought they should run the country. But Tyler pushed to take full control of the job.

Tyler had already served his home state of Virginia as governor, U.S. congressman, and U.S. senator. He was popular in the southern states because he believed that states should have more say about how they ran themselves. His stubbornness helped draw the lines that would later erupt into the Civil War. He helped Texas join the United States—as a slave state.

Tyler was the first president to become a widower while in office, and the first to remarry. His second wife, Julia, was thirty years younger. With his two wives, Tyler was father to fifteen children, the most of any U.S. president.

Just before the Civil War broke out, Tyler, broke, retired, and back at his farm in Virginia, tried to negotiate a peace treaty. But President Lincoln rejected all of his ideas. Tyler sided with the Confederacy and was elected to the Confederacy's Congress. He died a year later.

"Wealth can only be accumulated by the earnings of industry and the savings of frugality."

★ AT A GLANCE ★

BORN
March 29, 1790
Charles City County,
Virginia

POLITICAL PARTY
Democrat and Whig

FIRST LADIES
Letitia and Julia

CHILDREN
Mary, Robert, John, Letitia, Elizabeth, Anne, Alice, Tazewell, David, John, Julia, Lachlan, Lyon, Robert, and Pearl

PETS
Le Beau, a greyhound; The General, a horse

JAMES K. POLK
11th PRESIDENT ★ 1845 – 1849
Young Hickory

"No president who performs his duties faithfully and conscientiously can have any leisure."

★ AT A ★ GLANCE

BORN
November 2, 1795
Mecklenburg County,
North Carolina

POLITICAL PARTY
Democrat

VICE PRESIDENT
George M. Dallas

FIRST LADY
Sarah

PETS
Horses

James Polk believed that our country was destined to expand to the shores of the Pacific Ocean. This belief was called "Manifest Destiny." As Polk told Congress, "The people of this continent alone have the right to decide their own destiny."

Of course, this thinking caused problems, first with the British, who were still settling Canada. An argument broke out over where the U.S. borders were in the Pacific Northwest. As if playing a poker game, Polk started the slogan "54-40 or Fight!" meaning the latitude on the map that would be the border. It would have extended the United States way up into what today is Canada. When the British agreed to the more southerly 49th parallel, Polk was pleased.

On the southern border, problems started with Mexico over Texas. The Mexican War broke out and was never a fair fight. When it was over, the United States had not only secured Texas, but also the lands that would become parts of Arizona, California, Colorado, Nevada, New Mexico, Utah, and Wyoming. Polk did pay the Mexican government $15 million as compensation.

When he ran for president, Polk promised he would only serve one term and not try to get re-elected. He kept that promise. Polk left the country two-thirds larger than when he took office.

ZACHARY TAYLOR
12th PRESIDENT ★ 1849 – 1850
Old Rough and Ready

A hero of the Mexican-American War, General Zachary Taylor was one of the most popular men in the country, but had no experience in politics. He saw himself as a professional soldier, and soldiers, he believed, should not take sides in politics. He was called "Old Rough and Ready" because he shared the hardships of war with his men and dressed rather sloppily, wearing old farm clothes and a straw hat into battle.

When the Whig Party picked him to run for president, he didn't think he was qualified, but accepted because he felt it was his duty. He stepped right into the raging national argument over slavery: Should the new states of California, New Mexico, and Utah be admitted as slave or "free" states? When Taylor said that the new states should decide for themselves, both sides got mad at him.

Northern states wanted him to stop the spread of slavery. Southern states thought new non-slave states would make them less powerful, and they threatened to break away from the United States. Taylor warned them if they tried, he himself would lead the U.S. army against them.

Just sixteen months after becoming president, Taylor was at a Fourth of July ceremony laying the cornerstone of the Washington Monument. He collapsed from heat stroke after drinking a pitcher of water. He died five days later.

"For more than half a century, during which kingdoms and empires have fallen, this Union has stood unshaken."

★ AT A GLANCE ★

BORN
November 24, 1784
Near Barboursville,
Virginia

POLITICAL PARTY
Whig

VICE PRESIDENT
Millard Fillmore

FIRST LADY
Margaret

CHILDREN
Ann, Sarah, Octavia,
Margaret, Mary,
and Richard

PETS
Old Whitey, a horse

MILLARD FILLMORE
13th PRESIDENT ★ 1850 – 1853
Last of the Whigs

"May God save the country, for it is evident that the people will not."

★ AT A GLANCE ★

BORN
January 7, 1800
Summerhill, New York

POLITICAL PARTY
Whig

FIRST LADY
Abigail

CHILDREN
Millard and Mary

PETS
Founded Buffalo
chapter of ASPCA

Millard Fillmore became the second vice president to be promoted to president on the sudden death of a serving president.

Born poor in a log cabin on a farm near Ithaca, New York, Fillmore had to go to work instead of school to help feed his family. He taught himself to read and devoured every book he could get his hands on. A tall, handsome, and polite man, Fillmore later taught school and learned law working as a clerk. He served as a congressman and ran for governor of New York, but lost.

When he became president, the country was coming apart over the issue of slavery. Fillmore tried to hold it together by finding ways to keep both sides happy. He signed the Compromise of 1850, which, among other things, helped slave owners hunt down runaway slaves in northern states. The law enraged everyone who was against slavery and led Harriet Beecher Stowe to write the novel *Uncle Tom's Cabin,* a story about the horrors and injustice of slavery. The book turned many Americans against slavery once and for all.

It also helped lose Fillmore any chance of getting re-elected. One thing Fillmore does get credit for, however, was persuading Japan, who wanted nothing to do with us, to open its ports to U.S. ships and start trading with us. Fillmore and his wife also established the first permanent library at the White House.

FRANKLIN PIERCE
14th PRESIDENT ★ 1853 – 1857
Handsome Frank

Franklin Pierce went to college at Bowdoin in Maine and by his second year, he had the worst grades in his class. He eventually turned himself around, graduating third in a class that included Henry Wadsworth Longfellow and Nathaniel Hawthorne.

At 33, he became one of the youngest U.S. senators ever, but his wife, Jane, who was very strict and religious, hated the party-filled life of Washington, D.C. She made her husband resign and move back to New England. He joined the army as a private in the Mexican-American War and by the end of the war, he had been promoted to one-star general.

Just weeks before he was sworn in as president, his 11-year-old son, Benjamin, was killed in a train accident. The Pierces had already lost two other children. And so the first days and months in the White House were very sad for President and Mrs. Pierce.

Pierce tried to keep the peace between the North and the South, but he was never a very skilled politician. His biggest mistake was signing the Kansas–Nebraska Act, which set off deadly riots over slavery and seemed to hurry the country closer to the brink of civil war. He tried to buy Cuba, but Spain refused to sell. He did, however, add 29,000 square miles of land along the Mexican border. He was not nominated for a second term.

"With the Union my best and dearest earthly hopes are entwined."

★ AT A GLANCE ★

BORN
November 23, 1804
Hillsborough
(now Hillsboro), New Hampshire

POLITICAL PARTY
Democrat

VICE PRESIDENT
William R. D. King

FIRST LADY
Jane

CHILDREN
Franklin, Frank Robert, and Benjamin

JAMES BUCHANAN
15th PRESIDENT ★ 1857 – 1861
Old Buck

James Buchanan tried running for president three times before he finally won. And it couldn't have been at a worse time.

Two days into his term, the Supreme Court (mostly Southern judges) ruled that slaves are the property of their owners, not citizens, so they had no right to sue for their freedom. The Dred Scott Decision ignited fury among abolitionists, who wanted to abolish slavery.

Among them was John Brown, a radical abolitionist who tried to start a slave revolt by stealing weapons at Harpers Ferry, Virginia, and giving them to slaves. Brown was captured and hanged, but his death just made the abolitionists' cause grow stronger.

By 1861, eight Southern states had announced that they were leaving the United States and forming the Confederacy of American States where owning slaves would be legal. Buchanan condemned the states for leaving, but argued that he had no power to stop them.

Buchanan hated slavery. He actually bought slaves just to free them. But history blames him for not doing more to prevent the Civil War. On his last day in office, he sent a message to his successor: My dear sir, he wrote, if you are as happy on entering the Presidency as I am on leaving it, then you are a happy man indeed.

The man getting that letter was Abraham Lincoln.

"The test of leadership is not to put greatness into humanity, but to elicit it, for the greatness is already there."

★ AT A GLANCE ★

BORN
April 23, 1791
Cove Gap, Pennsylvania

POLITICAL PARTY
Democrat

VICE PRESIDENT
John C. Breckinridge

CHILDREN
Millard and Mary

PETS
Lara, a Newfoundland dog;
elephants from
the King of Siam; a pair of
American bald eagles

ABRAHAM LINCOLN
16th PRESIDENT ★ 1861 – 1865
Honest Abe

Growing up on the frontier, and as a self-taught country lawyer and politician, Abraham Lincoln spoke out against slavery his whole life. And, so, when he won the election in 1860, the pro-slavery Southern states saw what was coming. They left the Union and elected their own president, Jefferson Davis.

President Lincoln believed it was treason for the Southern states to quit the United States. He devoted himself to bringing the nation back together.

When Confederate troops fired on Fort Sumter in South Carolina in April 1861, Lincoln called out the army and the bloodiest chapter in American history began—The Civil War. More than 600,000 soldiers died over the next four years, but in the end, the Union won and slavery was abolished.

At six-foot-four, Lincoln was the tallest president.

Five days after the war ended, Lincoln and his wife went to see a play. John Wilkes Booth, an actor who favored the South, slipped into the theater, walked to the president's booth, and killed him with a pistol. Booth was hunted down and killed.

In his oath, Lincoln had promised to "preserve, protect, and defend" the United States. He kept that promise and for it, many people today believe he was our greatest president ever.

"Whenever I hear anyone arguing for slavery, I feel a strong impulse to see it tried on him personally."

★ AT A GLANCE ★

BORN
February 12, 1809
Hodgenville, Kentucky

POLITICAL PARTY
Whig and Republican

VICE PRESIDENTS
Hannibal Hamlin;
Andrew Johnson

FIRST LADY
Mary

CHILDREN
Robert, Edward, William,
and Thomas "Tad"

PETS
Old Bob, Lincoln's horse, who followed his hearse in his funeral; Fido, a yellow mutt

ANDREW JOHNSON
17th PRESIDENT ★ 1865 – 1869
The Veto President

"The goal to strive for is a poor government but a rich people."

★ AT A GLANCE ★

BORN
December 29, 1808
Raleigh, North Carolina

POLITICAL PARTY
Democrat and Unionist

FIRST LADY
Eliza

CHILDREN
Martha, Charles, Mary,
Robert, and Andrew

PETS
President Johnson
left food crumbs out
at night for a family
of mice living in
his walls.

When the Civil War broke out, Andrew Johnson, a senator from Tennessee, was the only Southern senator to stay at his job in Washington and not side with the South. Northerners loved him for it. It's not that he was against slavery, however (he owned slaves himself). He just believed the country should stay united. Lincoln rewarded him by making him vice president for his second term.

But if Lincoln was one of our best presidents, Johnson was one of the worst. Inheriting the huge job of rebuilding the country from the ashes of war, Johnson went right to work making a mess of it. While Congress was on vacation, he started handing out pardons by the thousands. He let the South set up something called "Black Codes," which were just new ways to keep African-Americans under white people. Then Johnson started to veto laws Congress passed to protect ex-slaves and even encouraged Southern governors not to cooperate with Congress.

Three years into his term, Congress had had enough and put him on trial, "impeached" him, for illegally firing a government worker.

He barely escaped getting kicked out of office by one vote. He left office a bitter man.

His administration is given credit for buying Alaska from Russia for $7 million.

ULYSSES S. GRANT
18th PRESIDENT ★ 1869 – 1877
Unconditional Surrender Grant

When the Civil War ended, General Ulysses S. Grant was a hero. He won the presidency in 1868, but his genius in war did not make him good at the ruthless style of warfare called politics.

Born Hiram Ulysses Grant, he was the son of a leather tanner and never had much interest in tanning or school. His father got him into West Point and because of a mix-up when he was signing in, they put his name down as Ulysses Simpson Grant. Grant preferred the name, since it echoed the initials of our country, so he kept it. His best subjects were horsemanship and math.

Grant fought in the Mexican War alongside his West Point classmate Robert E. Lee. Later he faced off against Lee in the Civil War. He accepted Lee's sword in surrender at Appomattox to end the Civil War.

As president, Grant was bewildered by the political process in Washington. Without realizing it, he let several dishonest men take advantage of his trust. One scandal after another rocked his two terms.

Learning that he was dying of cancer, Grant spent his last years writing his memoirs, with the help of Mark Twain. The book came out after he died, was an instant best seller, and made half a million dollars for his surviving family.

"I have never advocated war except as a means of peace."

★ AT A GLANCE ★

BORN
April 27, 1822
Point Pleasant, Ohio

POLITICAL PARTY
Republican

VICE PRESIDENTS
Schuyler Colfax;
Henry Wilson

FIRST LADY
Julia

CHILDREN
Frederick, Ulysses, Ellen,
and Jesse

PETS
Jeff Davis, Cincinnatus,
Egypt, St. Louis, Julia, Reb,
and Butcher Boy, all horses

RUTHERFORD B. HAYES
19th PRESIDENT ★ 1877 – 1881
Dark-Horse President

Rutherford Hayes was also a Union general in the Civil War. When he ran for president, he vowed he would only serve one term. That way he could focus on doing a good job and not worry about getting re-elected.

Winning the election, however, caused a scandal. In secret, his party bosses had to make shady deals and rig votes to get him elected. That's how he got the nickname "Rutherfraud."

But once in office he proved to be honest, upstanding, and hardworking. With the nation's wounds from the Civil War still healing, he had the last of the government troops removed from the South. He believed that education was the best way to prosperity and harmony among a free people.

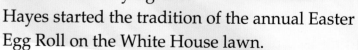

His wife, Lucy, was the first First Lady to have a college degree. When her husband was a general, she accompanied him to the battle camps and helped care for the wounded and dying. Mrs. Hayes started the tradition of the annual Easter Egg Roll on the White House lawn.

Thomas Edison demonstrated his new phonograph for the Hayeses—and they kept him up till three in the morning! Hayes was also the first president to try out a telephone. "An amazing invention," he said. "But who would ever want to use one?"

"He serves his party best who serves his country best."

★ AT A GLANCE ★

BORN
October 4, 1822
Delaware, Ohio

POLITICAL PARTY
Republican

VICE PRESIDENT
William Wheeler

FIRST LADY
Lucy

CHILDREN
Birchard, James, Rutherford, Joseph, George, Fanny, Scott, and Manning

PETS
Hector and Nellie, German shepherds; the first Siamese kitten in America

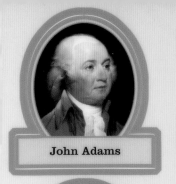
John Adams

John Quincy Adams

Chester A. Arthur

James Buchanan

George H. W. Bush

George W. Bush

Jimmy Carter

Grover Cleveland

Grover Cleveland

William Clinton

Calvin Coolidge

Dwight D. Eisenhower

Millard Fillmore

Gerald Ford

James A. Garfield

Ulysses S. Grant

Warren G. Harding

Benjamin Harrison

William Henry Harrison

Rutherford B. Hayes

Herbert Hoover

Andrew Jackson

Thomas Jefferson

Andrew Johnson

Lyndon B. Johnson

John F. Kennedy

Abraham Lincoln

James Madison

William McKinley

James Monroe

Richard Nixon

Barack Obama

Franklin Pierce

James K. Polk

Ronald Reagan

Franklin D. Roosevelt

Theodore Roosevelt

William Taft

Zachary Taylor

Harry S. Truman

John Tyler

Martin Van Buren

George Washington

Woodrow Wilson

JAMES A. GARFIELD
20th PRESIDENT ★ 1881
Preacher President

Probably the poorest person to ever become president, James Garfield was born in a log cabin and lost his father when he was just a year old. His mother struggled to raise the family.

When he was 17, Garfield worked on canal boats and put himself through school, eventually graduating from Williams College. He became a great teacher, preacher, and scholar. To amuse people, he could write in Greek with one hand and Latin with the other at the same time.

He was the first president to have his mother present at his swearing-in ceremony. She was a tiny, frail woman, and she moved into the White House with the First Family. Garfield, a six-foot-tall, ex-Civil War general used to personally carry his mother up and down the stairs.

As president, Garfield wanted to end the practice of handing out cushy government jobs as favors. Four months after Garfield took office, a deranged gunman, who had been turned down for a job, sneaked up on him in a train station and shot him in the back. The bullet lodged in Garfield's pancreas and doctors could not get it out. After two-and-a-half months of agonizing operations and infections, Garfield died, becoming the second U.S. president to be felled by an assassin's bullet. The gunman was tried and hanged. Garfield is seen as a martyr to the cause of honest government.

"A brave man is a man who dares to look the Devil in the face and tell him he is a Devil."

★ AT A GLANCE ★

BORN
November 19, 1831
Cuyahoga County, Ohio

POLITICAL PARTY
Republican

VICE PRESIDENT
Chester A. Arthur

FIRST LADY
Lucretia

CHILDREN
Eliza, Harry, James, Mary, Irvin, Abram, and Edward

PETS
Veto, a dog

25

CHESTER A. ARTHUR
21st PRESIDENT ★ 1881 – 1885
Elegant Arthur

"Good ballplayers make good citizens."

★ AT A GLANCE ★

BORN
October 5, 1829
Fairfield, Vermont

POLITICAL PARTY
Republican

FIRST LADY
Ellen
(died before her husband
became president)

CHILDREN
William, Chester,
and Ellen

**FAVORITE FOOD
AND WHISKERS**
Mutton chops

Chester Arthur was as shocked as anyone that President Garfield's assassin announced "Now Arthur is president!" after he gunned down Garfield.

Arthur never dreamed of becoming president. His biggest job before being vice president was running New York City's custom house, and there he was fired for "encouraging" employees to contribute money to his political party.

As president, Arthur turned over a new leaf and worked to make government honest. He turned his back on his old cronies who wanted jobs and instead supported laws that created a level playing field for getting government jobs. He also helped protect people from losing their jobs because of how they voted in political elections and what party they chose to join.

He built up our navy and got people to start thinking about preserving our nation's wildlife and wilderness.

Because he was a very fashionable dresser, he was called "Elegant Arthur." He was said to have more than eighty pairs of trousers and would change clothes several times a day, depending upon what he was doing.

He fiercely protected his personal life. "I may be president of the United States," he once said, "but my private life is nobody's business."

GROVER CLEVELAND
22nd & 24th PRESIDENT ★
1885-1889 & 1893 – 1897
Uncle Jumbo

Five years after the Civil War, Stephen Grover Cleveland, a hard-working young lawyer, was elected sheriff of Erie County, New York. The job included the role of executioner. He personally pulled the lever to hang two murderers.

At 250-plus pounds, Cleveland was a big, honest man, the kind that was good to have on your side. As sheriff, he was tireless, fair, and evenhanded, and was soon asked to run for mayor of Buffalo. He won, and before he knew it, he was governor of New York. He took on corrupt, dishonest people in government and exposed them. He became president at age 47.

"Honor lies in honest toil."

He was a president who stood up to Congress. "Backbone!" one man said. "He has so much of it, it makes him stick out in front!" Cleveland used his veto power to block Congress 584 times, more vetoes than all of the earlier presidents combined. By doing so, he paved the way for a more powerful presidency for the 20th century,

something for which future presidents would be grateful.

Cleveland was the only president to get married in the White House. His bride, Frances or "Frank," was thirty years younger, pretty, and extremely popular. They were the first presidential family to have a child born in the White House. The Baby Ruth candy bar was named after their daughter Ruth.

AT A GLANCE ★

BORN
March 18, 1837
Caldwell, New Jersey

POLITICAL PARTY
Democrat

VICE PRESIDENTS
Thomas A. Hendricks;
Adlai E. Stevenson

FIRST LADY
Frances "Frank"

CHILDREN
Ruth, Esther, Marion,
Richard, and Francis

PETS
Canaries, mockingbirds,
and a Japanese poodle

BENJAMIN HARRISON
23rd PRESIDENT ★ 1889 – 1893
The Human Iceberg

"The bud of victory is always in the truth."

He was named after his great-grandfather who signed the Declaration of Independence. His grandfather, William Henry Harrison, served as president for 30 days before dying in office. Other than that, Benjamin Harrison had few qualifications to be president of the United States.

He preferred books to people. He was so aloof and hard to talk to that people nicknamed him "the human iceberg." One of his rivals, Theodore Roosevelt, called him "a cold-blooded, narrow-minded, prejudiced, obstinate, timid, old psalm-singing Indianapolis politician."

But even though his bumbling with the economy probably helped bring on a depression, he did do some good things. He supported laws to make giant companies play fair, to protect forests, to reach out to the lands of the Pacific, especially Hawaii, and to build a canal through Central America to create a waterway between the Atlantic and Pacific oceans.

He was the first president to have electricity in the White House but after he got a shock, no one wanted to touch the switches and the lights would burn all night. He was also the first president to go to a baseball game (Reds 7, Senators 4; June 6, 1892). Still, when Harrison finished his term, he told his family he felt like he had just been released from prison.

28

WILLIAM McKINLEY
25th PRESIDENT ★ 1897 – 1901
The Major

The last president to have served in the Civil War and the first to ride in an automobile, William McKinley kept his Army rank as his nickname, "The Major," for the rest of his life.

When he became president, Cuba was a Spanish colony, but Cubans desperately wanted independence. Many Americans lived in Cuba and when riots broke out, McKinley sent the battleship Maine to Havana to protect the Americans. Three weeks later, the Maine exploded and sank. Even though the U.S. navy said it was an accident, America declared war on Spain and the Spanish-American War began.

Within four months, the United States had destroyed the Spanish fleet and taken control of Spain's global empire, including Cuba, Puerto Rico, the Philippines, Guam, and the Sandwich Islands (later renamed Hawaii).

McKinley picked a new vice president for his second term—a hero from the war and governor of New York, Theodore Roosevelt. Less than a year into his second term, McKinley was at a fair in Buffalo. A man with a bandaged hand stepped up and two shots rang out. A gun was hidden in the bandage! The president took both bullets in the chest. One week later, McKinley died from gangrene poisoning and Theodore Roosevelt was sworn in as twenty-sixth president of the United States.

"War should never be entered upon until every agency of peace has failed."

★ AT A GLANCE ★

BORN
January 29, 1843
Niles, Ohio

POLITICAL PARTY
Republican

VICE PRESIDENTS
Garret A. Hobart;
Theodore Roosevelt

FIRST LADY
Ida

CHILDREN
Katherine and Ida

PETS
Washington Post, a Mexican parrot, who could whistle "Yankee Doodle"

THEODORE ROOSEVELT
26th PRESIDENT ★ 1901 – 1909
T.R.

"It is no use to preach to [children] if you do not act decently yourself."

Born to a well-to-do New York family, Theodore Roosevelt was a scrawny and sickly asthmatic boy who was picked on at school. With his father's help, he soon discovered the benefits of hard exercise and by the time he was a teenager, he was strong enough to box and wrestle at Harvard College. He graduated, married, and entered politics.

Then tragedy struck. On the same day, in the same house, his wife and his mother both died within hours of each other. Theodore went out to the Western frontier to recover from his grief. He herded cattle, hunted grizzlies, and even chased outlaws.

After two years he returned to New York and married a childhood sweetheart, Edith, and got back into public service. When the Spanish-American War broke out, Roosevelt put together a hand-picked elite cavalry unit called the Rough Riders. In a daring raid, they took San Juan Hill in Cuba and became heroes.

As president, he filled the job vigorously with his own ideals and vision. He believed that ordinary people should not be cheated by big companies. The first environmentalist president, he set aside nearly 200 million acres for national forests, reserves, and wildlife refuges. (The "Teddy Bear" is named after him.) He was also given the Nobel Peace Prize for helping to stop the war between Russia and Japan.

WILLIAM HOWARD TAFT
27th PRESIDENT ★ 1909 – 1913
Big Bill

Young Bill Taft's parents put a lot of pressure on him growing up. His father had been President Grant's attorney general and great things were expected of his son. Some historians suggest that this pressure had something to do with Taft's extraordinary weight.

Taft weighed in at about 332 pounds. He had to have a new bathtub installed (he got stuck in the old one and it took six men to pull him out). People joked about his size. "That Taft is a real gentleman," said one. "He got up on a streetcar and gave his seat to three ladies."

But Taft got good things done. He made big businesses get in line, established the post office system, and set up the income tax system.

A great lover of baseball as a boy (big hitter but not a great base runner), Taft established the tradition of presidents throwing out the first pitch to start the season. He was also the first president to play golf, and a lot of his critics thought he should spend more time at his desk and less on the links.

His real dream in life was to be chief justice of the Supreme Court, and that job he would get eight years after leaving the White House. "It is very difficult for me to understand," said one judge, "how a man who is so good as chief justice could have been so bad as president."

"Politics, when I am in it, makes me sick."

★ AT A GLANCE ★

BORN
September 15, 1857
Cincinnati, Ohio

POLITICAL PARTY
Republican

VICE PRESIDENT
James S. Sherman

FIRST LADY
Helen "Nellie"

CHILDREN
Robert, Helen,
and Charles

PETS
Pauline, the last milk cow
kept at the White House

WOODROW WILSON
28th PRESIDENT ★ 1913 – 1921
Professor

The son of a minister, Woodrow Wilson had a reading disorder and struggled to overcome it. He started off as a lawyer, but got bored, and became a history professor. He ended up head of Princeton University and had a reputation for honesty. Democrats asked him to run for governor of New Jersey, and then for president.

As president, he took on many big issues that affected everyone—child labor, the eight-hour workday, the right to strike, and women's right to vote.

When World War I broke out in Europe, Wilson tried to keep America out of it. But when German subs kept threatening our ships, he had no choice. Once in the war, he threw the full might of America at the enemy, hurrying a victory. At the same time, he worked around the clock to find a way to get lasting peace out of the sacrifice (10 million soldiers died at a cost of $300 billion). He wanted World War I to be the war that ended war for good.

With that in mind, he suggested the world create an organization where every nation would have a seat at the table to talk things out before going to war. He couldn't get Congress to approve it. Years later, the idea would be reborn as the United Nations.

"I not only use all the brains that I have, but all that I can borrow."

★ AT A GLANCE ★

BORN
December 29, 1856
Staunton, Virginia

POLITICAL PARTY
Democrat

VICE PRESIDENT
Thomas R. Marshall

FIRST LADIES
Ellen (died 1914)
and Edith (married 1915)

CHILDREN
Margaret, Jessie,
and Eleanor

PETS
Old Ike, a ram that chewed
cigars and kept the White
House lawn trimmed

WARREN HARDING
29th PRESIDENT ★ 1921 – 1923
Wobbly Warren

Called by many America's worst president, Warren Harding worked hard to earn the title. His campaign slogan was "Back to Normalcy," inviting Americans to turn back the clock to the simpler times before World War I—and all the preachy lectures from the high-minded "Professor," Woodrow Wilson.

"I'm not fit for this office and never should have been here."

Unfortunately, America took him up on it. Harding won by a landslide. Once in office, Harding realized he really didn't know what the job of president was. Harding acted as if all he had to do was look and act presidential, avoiding any big issues. "I don't know what to do or where to go," he told a friend. "There must be a book that talks all about it."

Luckily he had appointed three or four good, men to his cabinet, who kept the country from falling apart. Men like Calvin Coolidge, Andrew Mellon, Charles Evans Hughes, and Herbert Hoover. Still, the good-natured and trusting "Wobbly Warren" let a gang of dishonest scoundrels into his administration, and they took bribes and broke laws to make themselves rich.

When these no-goods were about to be brought to trial, one fled the country, two committed suicide, and Harding, on a trip to Alaska, got sick from what seemed to be food poisoning. He soon died of heart failure. People immediately started to suspect that he had been murdered.

★ AT A GLANCE ★

BORN
November 2, 1865
Blooming Grove, Ohio

POLITICAL PARTY
Republican

VICE PRESIDENT
Calvin Coolidge

FIRST LADY
Florence "Duchess"

CHILDREN
Marshall Eugene DeWolfe

PETS
Laddie Boy,
an Airedale terrier;
Old Boy,
an English bulldog;
canaries

CALVIN COOLIDGE
30th PRESIDENT ★ 1923 – 1929
Silent Cal

"Any man who does not like dogs and want them about, does not deserve to be in the White House."

★ AT A ★ GLANCE

BORN
July 4, 1872
Plymouth Notch, Vermont

POLITICAL PARTY
Republican

VICE PRESIDENT
Charles Gates Dawes

FIRST LADY
Grace

CHILDREN
John and Calvin

PETS
Rebecca and Rueben, raccoons; Palo Alto, King Cole, Blackberry, Rough, Ruby, Boston Beans, and many more dogs

V ice President Calvin Coolidge was visiting his father in Vermont when President Harding died. News reached them at night and Coolidge's father, a justice of the peace, administered the oath of office to his son, who immediately went back to bed.

A quiet, witty New Englander, Coolidge was the kind of calm and wholesome leader the country needed after Harding's escapades. During his term, the country was going through good times, often called the Roaring Twenties. Coolidge's thinking was to leave well enough alone. He gave tax cuts to the rich and did little to help farmers who were going out of business. The stock market got hotter and hotter, worrying many that it was getting too hot and people were risking too much. His answer was that it wasn't the president's job to try to control it.

He slept more than any president, about ten hours a day, including afternoon naps. But many think he was also asleep at the switch and his leave-well-enough-alone approach to being president set the stage for the disaster that was to follow.

"Silent Cal" was famous for not talking. Once a high-society lady seated next to him said, "You must talk to me, Mr. Coolidge. I made a bet today that I could get more than two words out of you." Coolidge replied: "You lose."

HERBERT C. HOOVER
31st PRESIDENT ★ 1929 – 1933
Chief

When Herbert Hoover was born, his father, a blacksmith, had such high hopes he marched through town announcing, "We have another General Grant in our house!"

"Bert" Hoover grew up in Iowa, where he learned how to trap rabbits in a cracker box and catch fish with a willow rod, butcher's string, and hooks—ten for a dime. When he was 6, his father died. His mother died four years later and Bert was sent to live with an uncle in Oregon.

Hoover went to Stanford, the new, free college in California, studying geology and mining. Before long, he was a self-made millionaire, traveling the world over. He was very popular when he ran for president and won easily. But a few months later, the stock market crashed and the Great Depression began. Banks had no money, people lost their jobs, and everyone blamed Hoover. None of what he tried to do improved things and by the time his term was ending, 14 million people were without work and many lived in shacks and tent villages in extreme poverty.

Although history has judged Hoover a poor president, he was a great humanitarian. After World War II, he helped get food to the needy of war-torn Europe. For 25 years he ran the Boys Clubs of America, because he always had special concern for "the boys of the city streets."

"Children are our most valuable natural resource."

AT A GLANCE

BORN
August 10, 1874
West Branch, Iowa

POLITICAL PARTY
Republican

VICE PRESIDENT
Charles Curtis

FIRST LADY
Lou

CHILDREN
Herbert and Allan

PETS
Patrick, an Irish wolfhound; Sonnie and Big Ben, fox terriers; Yukon, an Eskimo dog; two alligators that wandered around the White House

FRANKLIN D. ROOSEVELT
32nd PRESIDENT ★ 1933 – 1945
FDR

"When you get to the end of your rope, tie a knot and hang on."

When Franklin Roosevelt became president, millions of Americans were out of work, poor, and homeless. And there was no end in sight to their misery and suffering. In his first speech, FDR gave hope. "This great Nation will endure as it has endured, will revive, and will prosper. The only thing we have to fear is fear itself."

He charged into the job, starting many programs that gave people a "new deal" and put them to work. After four years, things seemed to be improving, and he won re-election. In his second term, however, war broke out in Europe when Hitler's Nazi Germany invaded Poland.

When the Japanese attacked our ships anchored at Pearl Harbor, Hawaii, we entered World War II and fought it for the next four years. FDR was a true commander-in-chief, studying battle plans, appointing field commanders, and using the radio to talk to Americans. He kept the nation solidly behind the war.

FDR became the only U.S. president to win four straight elections. When he died suddenly of a brain hemorrhage, the country was at work again, victory in the Second World War was just around the corner, and the United States had a new place of respect in the world. He died as one of the most beloved, admired, and respected leaders in history.

HARRY S. TRUMAN
33rd PRESIDENT ★ 1945 – 1953
Give 'Em Hell Harry

Three months after Harry Truman became vice president, he became president. It felt like "the moon, the stars, and all the planets had fallen on me," he said.

President Truman was immediately faced with a decision more awesome than any president had ever faced before. American scientists had created a new weapon—a new kind of bomb— the likes of which the world had never seen. Its destructive power was truly terrifying.

If Truman had let the war drag on, we would have had to invade Japan at a cost of hundreds of thousands of lives. If we used the bomb, Japan would have to surrender, and all those lives would be spared. Truman dropped two atomic bombs on Japan and the war came to an end within days.

But the challenges now were to take care of all the soldiers coming home and to help rebuild the world. Truman saw that Communism was spreading from the Soviet Union and he put the United States right in its way. This "Cold War" would occupy U.S. presidents for the next thirty years. Truman sent troops to Korea.

Truman was a devoted family man. His daughter, Margaret, was a singer and when a newspaper writer criticized her, President Truman wrote, "Someday I hope to meet you. When that happens, you'll need a new nose…."

"The best way to give advice to your children is to find out what they want and then advise them to do it."

★ **AT A GLANCE** ★

BORN
May 8, 1884
Lamar, Missouri

POLITICAL PARTY
Democrat

VICE PRESIDENT
Alben William Barkley

FIRST LADY
Elizabeth "Bess"

CHILD
Margaret

PETS
Feller,
the unwanted dog;
Mike, Margaret's
Irish setter

DWIGHT D. EISENHOWER
34th PRESIDENT ★ 1953 – 1961
Ike

"Only Americans can hurt America."

★ AT A ★ GLANCE

BORN
October 14, 1890
Denison, Texas

POLITICAL PARTY
Republican

VICE PRESIDENT
Richard M. Nixon

FIRST LADY
Marie "Mamie"

CHILDREN
Doud Dwight and John

PET
Heidi, a Weimaraner

Growing up with five brothers, "Ike" Eisenhower knew how to fight—and how to make peace. One of America's greatest military commanders, Five-star General Dwight D. Eisenhower gave the order to launch Operation

Overlord, or D-Day, the start of the freeing of Europe from Nazism during World War II.

When he came home, he was such a hero that President Truman suggested to him that they run together in 1948—but with Eisenhower as president and Truman as vice president! Instead, Eisenhower became president of Columbia University and ran for the White House as a Republican in 1952. Campaign buttons read: "I like Ike!" And a lot of people did. He won in a landslide.

Eisenhower ended the war in Korea but continued to oppose the spread of Communism across the world. He also worked for cooperation between people at home. When riots broke out over African-American schoolchildren being allowed into white schools in Little Rock, Arkansas, Eisenhower sent troops to keep the peace—and escort the children into the schools.

Eisenhower's favorite activity was golf. He had a putting green installed behind the White House so he could practice.

Ike left office as one of the best-liked presidents ever.

JOHN F. KENNEDY
35th PRESIDENT ★ 1961 – 1963
Jack

President for only 1,000 days, Jack Kennedy left one of the most lasting impressions of any president. Handsome, charming, and eloquent as an actor, he inspired a whole generation to take up the challenges of a "New Frontier."

Born into a rich family, Kennedy was captain of a small PT (patrol torpedo) boat in the

Pacific during World War II. One night, while the boat drifted and the crew slept, a Japanese destroyer rammed the boat and the whole crew went into the water. Kennedy led his men on a three-mile swim through shark-infested waters to safety, towing a wounded crewman by holding the strap from his life vest in his teeth.

Kennedy came home a hero and went into politics. After serving in Congress, he became the youngest man ever to run for president and won. He told Americans to "ask not what your country can do for you—ask what you can do for your country."

He passed a law giving equal rights to minorities. He promised to put a man on the moon within nine years (it came true). He also started putting troops into a small Asian country called Vietnam.

In an event that still shocks the world, Kennedy was assassinated by gunman Lee Harvey Oswald in Dallas on November 22, 1963.

"Man is still the most extraordinary computer of all."

★ AT A GLANCE ★

BORN
May 29, 1917
Brookline, Massachusetts

POLITICAL PARTY
Democrat

VICE PRESIDENT
Lyndon B. Johnson

FIRST LADY
Jacqueline "Jackie"

CHILDREN
Caroline, John Jr.,
and Patrick
(died in infancy)

PETS
Charlie, a Welsh terrier;
Tom Kitten, a cat;
Macaroni, Caroline's pony;
Zsa Zsa, a rabbit;
Sardar, a horse

LYNDON B. JOHNSON
36th PRESIDENT ★ 1963 – 1969
LBJ

"You aren't learning anything when you're talking."

★ AT A ★ GLANCE

BORN
August 27, 1908
Stonewall, Texas

POLITICAL PARTY
Democrat

VICE PRESIDENTS
Hubert H. Humphrey

FIRST LADY
Claudia "Lady Bird"

CHILDREN
Lynda Bird and
Luci Baines

PETS
Beagles, a collie;
Yuki, a stray mutt
found in a gas station
and adopted

The first president ever sworn into office aboard an airplane, Lyndon Johnson asked the country to honor President Kennedy's memory by continuing the good work he started. We would create "The Great Society," he said. We would end racial hatred, clean up our air and water, and most important of all, declare an all-out "war on poverty."

Johnson, or "LBJ," was a big, no-nonsense Texan who spoke with a drawl and often wore a Stetson cowboy hat. He was very good at politics and got many of his Great Society ideas put into law, making him popular and winning him the next election easily.

But the war in Vietnam was out of control and dividing Americans against each other. The poor, minorities, and anti-war protesters were fed up and were holding demonstrations across the country. Many got violent. It was one of the most turbulent times in our history.

By the time Johnson was up for re-election, there were a half-million U.S. soldiers in Vietnam with casualties rising. We had dropped more bombs there than we had in all of Europe in World War II. And no victory was in sight.

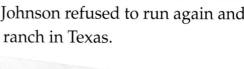

Discouraged and with a heavy heart, Johnson refused to run again and retired to his ranch in Texas.

RICHARD M. NIXON
37th PRESIDENT ★ 1969 – 1974
Tricky Dick

The son of a grocer, Richard Nixon was the first president to speak with a man on the moon, and the first president to resign from office.

Nixon's rise in politics was like a meteor: congressman in 1946, senator in 1950, vice president in 1952. If it had not been for a few votes in 1960, he would have beaten Kennedy and been the 35th president.

"I am not a crook."

Nixon came back and won the presidency in 1968. He was very clever when it came to getting votes. Some said too clever and gave him the nickname "Tricky Dick." He got elected president by promising to end the war in Vietnam, but the war dragged on and on.

He brought some troops home, but increased the bombing. "Peace is at hand," the White House kept saying, but 20,000 more Americans died before the U.S. got out of Vietnam completely.

To his credit, Nixon did start talking with the Communist giants China and the Soviet Union, but his "tricks" caught up with him.

Running for re-election in 1972, he was to win by a mile. But, wanting to be sure, his assistants had been spying on the competition. When his spies were caught, most of them lied. So did Nixon. He resigned in disgrace rather than be impeached—put on trial—by the Senate.

★ **AT A GLANCE** ★

BORN
January 9, 1913
Yorba Linda, California

POLITICAL PARTY
Republican

VICE PRESIDENTS
Spiro T. Agnew;
Gerald R. Ford

FIRST LADY
Thelma "Pat"

CHILDREN
Patricia "Tricia" and Julie

PETS
Checkers, a spaniel;
Vicky, a poodle;
Pasha, a terrier;
King Timahoe,
an Irish setter

GERALD R. FORD
38th PRESIDENT ★ 1974 – 1977
Jerry

"I am a Ford, not a Lincoln."

★ AT A GLANCE ★

BORN
July 14, 1913
Omaha, Nebraska

POLITICAL PARTY
Republican

VICE PRESIDENT
Nelson A. Rockefeller

FIRST LADY
Elizabeth Anne "Betty"

CHILDREN
Michael, John, Steven,
and Susan

PET
Liberty,
a golden retriever,
who gave birth to a
litter of puppies
in the White House

Jerry Ford became president when Richard Nixon resigned in disgrace. "My fellow Americans," he said, entering the White House. "Our long national nightmare is over." He made it his goal to restore people's faith in the presidency.

And he knew something about scoring goals. A star football player, he was an All-American center and linebacker for the Michigan Wolverines and led them to two undefeated, championship seasons. Later he went to Yale Law School and paid his tuition by coaching Yale's JV football team.

Ford served on an aircraft carrier in World War II and then became a congressman and served for twenty-five years. His biggest hope was to be Speaker of the House, but he had to settle for vice president and then president.

By pardoning Richard Nixon, Ford ruined his chances for continuing as president. Some people thought something fishy was going on. But Ford did it, he said, because it was the right thing to do, to help heal the country.

Ford often said that the thing he was proudest of was making Eagle in the Boy Scouts. He kept a Boy Scout manual on his desk throughout his career. When he died in 2006, 400 Eagle Scouts formed an honor guard at his funeral. His wife Betty also won praise helping people overcome dependencies on drugs and alcohol.

JIMMY CARTER
39th PRESIDENT ★ 1977 – 1981
Jimbo

Jimmy Carter grew up on his family's peanut farm in Georgia. He studied nuclear physics at the U.S. Naval Academy at Annapolis and worked as an engineer running the engines on a nuclear submarine. When his father died in 1953, Jimmy went home to run the farm and soon got into politics, rising to governor of Georgia.

When he ran for president, people liked him because he was an "outsider" in Washington. Voters, tired of wheelers and dealers in the government, wanted someone new.

However, there was a global energy crisis going on—gas prices skyrocketed. Cars had to wait in long lines just to buy gas. It got more expensive to borrow money to buy a house.

In Iran, protesters stormed our embassy and took 52 U.S. diplomats hostage and held them as prisoners for 444 days. Carter worked around the clock to get them free, but couldn't.

Not being a Washington "insider" worked against Carter. He had trouble getting Congress to go along with him on many of his ideas to solve these problems. And things just didn't seem to get any better. He lost re-election.

An intelligent, decent, and sincere man, Carter was the third U.S. president to be awarded a Nobel Peace Prize, in his case, for forging a peace treaty between warring sides in the Middle East.

"Wherever life takes us, there are always moments of wonder."

★ AT A GLANCE ★

BORN
October 1, 1924
Plains, Georgia

POLITICAL PARTY
Democrat

VICE PRESIDENT
Walter Mondale

FIRST LADY
Rosalynn

CHILDREN
John "Jack,"
James Earl III "Chip,"
Jeffrey "Jeff," and Amy

PETS
Grits, a collie;
Misty Malarky
Ying Yang,
a Siamese cat

RONALD REAGAN
40th PRESIDENT ★ 1981 – 1989
The Great Communicator

"Don't be afraid to see what you see."

★ **AT A GLANCE** ★

BORN
February 6, 1911
Tampico, Illinois

POLITICAL PARTY
Republican

VICE PRESIDENT
George H. W. Bush

FIRST LADY
Nancy

CHILDREN
Maureen, Michael,
Patricia, and Ronald

PETS
Lucky, a Bouvier des
Flandres; Rex,
a King Charles spaniel

At 69, former movie star Ronald Reagan was the oldest president ever to enter the White House. Called the Great Communicator, Reagan was perfectly at ease in front of cameras and large crowds. His years in Hollywood had prepared him for one of the greatest demands of the job: winning people over.

He made more than fifty movies for Warner Brothers Studios, usually cast as the wholesome All-American kid. He then went to work for General Electric as a television host and became familiar to even more Americans.

When he entered politics, he rose quickly, serving as governor of California for eight years. Running for president, his message was that government was too big and reducing taxes for the rich would help everyone when their wealth "trickled down" to the less wealthy. Instead of economics, critics called it Reaganomics.

Bringing America Back!

Shortly after he took office, a deranged gunman tried to assassinate him outside of a hotel in Washington, D.C. He was wounded, but returned to office a short time later.

Reagan will be remembered for hurrying the end of the Cold War and for trying to make the government work better. "I have wondered at times," he said, "what the Ten Commandments would have looked like if Moses had run them through the U.S. Congress."

GEORGE H.W. BUSH
41st PRESIDENT ★ 1989 – 1993
Poppy

George Bush put off going to college and joined the military during World War II. He was the youngest pilot in the Navy and flew 58 combat missions in the Pacific. He won the Distinguished Flying Cross for bravery. He came home, graduated with honors from Yale, worked in the oil business, then got into politics.

By the time Ronald Reagan picked him to run as vice president, Bush had served in several top government jobs, including head of the Central Intelligence Agency, or CIA.

As vice president, he organized all branches of the military to cooperate and try to stop the flow of illegal drugs into our country. Code-named Operation Blue Lightning, it equipped jets, speed boats, and helicopters with state-of-the-art sensors and tracking devices to snag drug smugglers as they tried to land on our shores.

In 1988, George Bush became the first vice president elected to president since Martin Van Buren in 1836.

When Iraq invaded Kuwait, he sent a force into the Persian Gulf and drove back Saddam Hussein's invasion. He was popular for a while, but the sagging economy prevented him from getting re-elected.

"We are not the sum of our possessions."

★ AT A GLANCE ★

BORN
June 12, 1924
Milton, Massachusetts

POLITICAL PARTY
Republican

VICE PRESIDENT
J. Danforth ("Dan") Quayle

FIRST LADY
Barbara

CHILDREN
George W., Robin,
John Ellis "Jeb," Neil,
Marvin, and Dorothy

PET
Millie, a springer spaniel

WILLIAM J. CLINTON
42nd PRESIDENT ★ 1993 – 2001
Slick Willie

"There is nothing wrong with America that cannot be cured by what is right with America."

★ AT A GLANCE ★

BORN
August 19, 1946
Hope, Arkansas

POLITICAL PARTY
Democrat

VICE PRESIDENT
Albert Gore

FIRST LADY
Hillary Rodham

CHILD
Chelsea Victoria

PETS
Socks, a cat;
Buddy, a dog

When Bill Clinton was 16, he was an elected delegate to Boys Nation, a youth organization. The group gathered in Washington, D.C. where he met and shook hands with President John F. Kennedy. From then on, he said, Kennedy was his hero and role model.

A bright student, Clinton studied at Oxford University as a Rhodes scholar and graduated from Yale Law School. At the age of 32, he became the governor of Arkansas, the youngest governor in the country. He was elected president fourteen years later.

As president, Clinton gained respect in foreign countries, especially for helping to end conflict in central Europe. And he helped the economy at home. He relaxed by playing the saxophone, playing the card game Hearts, and doing crossword puzzles. He was the first Democratic president elected to a second term since FDR.

But Clinton became only the second president to be impeached—or put on trial—by the Senate for misbehavior in office. Still, he remained a very strong and powerful spokesman for the Democratic Party. His wife, Hillary Rodham, went on to make history, becoming the first ever ex-First Lady to run for the U.S. Senate and win, and the first ex-First Lady to announce that she would run for president.

GEORGE W. BUSH
43rd PRESIDENT ★ 2001 – 2009
W. (Dubya)

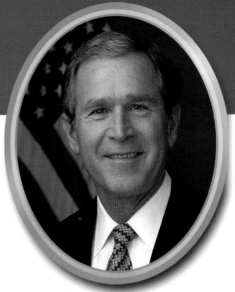

The 2000 presidential election was so close, it took forty extra days to count all the votes. Finally, the Supreme Court had to decide which of the candidates—Al Gore or George W. Bush—had actually won it. When the high court voted 5-to-4 that Bush was the winner, it was only the second time in history that a former president's son had won the office himself. (John Quincy Adams was the first, 175 years earlier.)

Born in Connecticut, he moved as a toddler to Texas. George "W." went to Yale and then Harvard Business School, after flying fighter jets for the Air National Guard. Later he was elected governor of Texas.

As president, Bush wanted to lower taxes and improve education, but history stepped in and shifted his focus. On September 11, 2001, terrorists hijacked planes and crashed them into New York's World Trade Center and the Pentagon in Virginia. President Bush soon declared war on terrorism. He created the Department of Homeland Security and sent our forces to invade Afghanistan. Later he convinced Congress to authorize an invasion of Iraq.

"America was targeted for attack," he said, "because we are the brightest beacon for freedom and opportunity in the world. And no one will keep that light from shining."

"America will never seek a permission slip to defend the security of our people."

★ AT A ★ GLANCE

BORN
July 6, 1946
New Haven, Connecticut

POLITICAL PARTY
Republican

VICE PRESIDENT
Richard Cheney

FIRST LADY
Laura

CHILDREN
Barbara and Jenna
(twins)

PETS
Miss Beazley
and Barney,
Scottish terriers;
India, a cat

BARACK OBAMA
44th PRESIDENT ★ 2009 –
Barry

"Change will not come if we wait for some other person, or if we wait for some other time. We are the ones we've been waiting for. We are the change that we seek. "

★ AT A GLANCE ★

BORN
August 4, 1961
Honolulu, Hawaii

POLITICAL PARTY
Democrat

VICE PRESIDENTS
Joe Biden

FIRST LADY
Michelle

CHILDREN
Malia and Sasha

PET
Bo, a Portuguese
water dog

When Barack Obama took office in 2009, he already faced major challenges. America was fighting two wars and the economy was in meltdown. Unemployment was on the rise, and Congress was deeply divided on issues like immigration, taxes, and health care. Obama had campaigned on a promise of "Change we can believe in." He would soon learn that change in Washington does not come easily.

Born in Honolulu, Hawaii, Obama learned to appreciate Hawaii's multi-racial society as he grew up. "The opportunity that Hawaii offered—to experience a variety of cultures in a climate of mutual respect—became a basis of my world view, and a basis for the values I hold most dear."

He began his political career as an Illinois State Senator. In 2004, he won a seat in the U.S. Senate. When Obama delivered the keynote speech at the 2004 Democratic convention nine million people watched it, boosting his national profile. In 2008, he defeated John McCain in the general election to become America's first African-American president.

As the 2012 presidential election approached, Obama faced many of the same challenges he did in 2009. He also faced a field of Republican presidential hopefuls, all with a common goal: make Obama a one-term president. The voters, of course, would have the final say.